Selah

Ivania,
Thank you for
being a beautiful human.
I hope you get
messages.

Published by
Tiffany Banks

ISBN-13: 9780692932520

Cover photo taken by Saréya Shorter

Dedicated to Mike…
I lived one of my worse nightmares,
but have awakened to understand that
I never lost you.

Azurite

Cleanses the mind and soul. Initiates transformation

December 2, 2004

Fall

Iniquities
On a fall bitten tree
Longing for a wind
To blow them away
Please let the season change
Each leaf—dead
Hanging on a branch
A past season
Which grew cold dying
Now in need of life
Shedding…
Growth…

May 10, 2007

Black Rain

A cloud—black
The earth, anxious for rain
Under God—a roof
Warring to believe such an entity can
be—can heal
The desolation, the fracture...
He walks out the door
An echo of words run out of sound
My face stained
Fighting my need to make sense of
prayer I do it,
Earnestly

For Duane

One of the best gifts in life is when the
body finally learns to respect the soul
For whatever reason, right now, is
your time to ascend
But we petition God
To leave us with just a bit—a piece of
you
That piece of you that's set apart from
a crowd, but still in it
The light of your smile, which
everyone in this room has the most
trouble letting go of,
Your charismatic aura,
And ability to bring a good vibe into
any space
You were one of the good guys
Thank you for leaving this world with
your seed
When gems like you leave the earth, it
broadens the perspective
Of the ones who watch them go
It reminds us that
Love is action
That time, is limited

That connectivity, is divine
That people—friends and family, are
not disposable
And that nothing and no one is bigger
than God
It is no surprise that this room would
be full,
As we are all trying to understand why
out of everyone it is *your* time
And all that registers is;
That no one knows when it's their
time,
Therefore live like it could be any
second
Not with fear
But with gratitude
And although you didn't know that you
would leave
You knew to live
Some people go and leave an
example of how not to perish
But others like you leave a mark
Teaching us how you treaded upon
this soil
You made for us a wrapped gift of
your legacy,
Which expands upon your departure

As the sun greets us with new chance
and opportunity
We know for you its rays have set for
the last time
But only as you have broken out of
your cocoon
Into an infinite being stronger than
even the sun's universal power
You've led us into prayer
We find joy inside this hurt
You've left seed on good ground for
purpose
You've left... love
You had plans as a child
You had plans as a man
You had plans as a father
And like the bloom of a cherry
blossom,
Even in cold conditions,
Consider your plans accomplished
Death is only to the body
Rest in paradise

Agate

*Strength stone—courage and strength
for both mind and body*

Resurrected

In the moment of realizing and
changing,
That I had been dependent
On your tangibility,
I came back to life

2007

No pity parties

Raindrops washed out the black
leaves inside me
Refuge—a woman's place of solitude
Liberated, wisdom, now is what leads
Praise! The spiritual mind is the tool
Tears, confusion, humiliation, fear
All shot towards me—no honor in love
All cried out, authority drew God near
Spirit things, a fight in me from above
Infinite dimensions, some, growing
seeds
All design this unique make-up and
frame
Fought devils, flew with angels, now,
love me
Seven strong earth-stones spell and
paint my name
Golden waves wash and wisdom
strokes my face
It's my playground! In spirit win these
games

Go For It

The elevator doors open and you step onto the seventh floor of the old multi-purpose building. The smell of new paint and stale air aggressively greets you. You stop right there, and the elevator doors behind you close. You don't see any signs of where to sign in. You look across the narrow hallway where flat coffee brown carpet usher your view up towards nothing. You breathe in deeply, and walk to your left out toward another hallway entry. There it is, a sign, handwritten, reading, "AUDITIONS" with an arrow pointing left. Your chest thumps. You capture another deep breath. This time holding it in slightly longer, begging it to save you from the war in your chest. Another sign and you turn right. There's still no sign of others. You start to hope that it is cancelled, but another sign points you to the right again. You walk faster and your palms sweat. You wish someone were with you. You consider your mom, but instantly feel relief that she won't be here to say she's right about your lack of potential to "make it," in case you mess up. After practice once when you were 10, you showed your mom how good your demi-pointe was. She did not congratulate you. She never did.

"When I was your age, I was mastering my en pointe" she told you. "Mrs. Landa told me that mine was very strong. She had me show all the other students and their parents."

"Like I said, I was past what she is showing you at your age," she grunted.

From then on, you rarely came home to show her anything new that you'd learned.

You hear chatter now. You're forced by the end of the hallway to make another right.

There are girls around the same age as you fiddling around in line. Against the wall is a rectangular table where two older women take information for registration. You observe the other girls, they seem relaxed. They seem to know one another. You ask the girl in front of you to confirm the time of the audition. Agitated, she asks you to repeat yourself and you do so reluctantly, taken by her rudeness. "3," she replies, flatly. You think that you can make a friend and get through this with someone, but all the other girls in that hallway give you the same empty eye contact.

The double doors to the studio are heavy. You use your bodyweight to enter. Every wall in the room is covered from top to bottom with mirrors. Girls line every wall against the barre. To the right of the doors is where a long table with four empty chairs is. You swallow as hard as you can. Your eyes scramble to find a post. All of the other girls wear their hair like you in a mid-high bun. Yours is smooth, dark, tied tightly, and not one hair out of place. The scalp in the back of your neck is sore. You look around observing what everyone else is doing. You find refuge from the awkwardness at the edge of the mirrored wall in the corner. You grab hold of the barre, then transition to the floor to stretch your back and legs, but when you realize no other girls are on the floor you scurry back up, unsure if you are following the etiquette for such a setting.

The double doors screech open yielding to four people; three women and one man. They do not look at anyone in the room and uniformly proceed to the table, each claiming a chair. The man is wearing a white collared shirt, black slacks, and a black blazer. His toupee' sits symmetrically on top of his head. The women are wearing dresses which go below the knee. All dark tones navy, black, and a deep purple. The four are expressionless and ridged. They own

their posts organizing notebooks and cards.

Thumps in your chest return with

vengeance. Your stomach turns as you go over

in your head the critiques that your mom had

given you over the years. Is this what she said

you wouldn't measure up to? You feel paralyzed.

You look around searching for someone, anyone

of the other girls to make eye contact with in

hopes of sharing the intensity. But none of them

offers warmth, just an icy barricade.

Returning your attention to the barre

and the mirror behind it, you study yourself. You

remember your mom's mirror with "ugly" and

"hate myself" written in red lipstick across it. The writing stayed for months. In that mirror she cut her hair into a frizzed boy-cut using her boyfriend Roy's shears. You never got to know him because he only came around after she thought you had gone to sleep. Red lipstick flashes onto the mirror in front of you now and you grow alert blinking the writing away. You start warming up with your demi-plié, knees slightly bending over your toes. Eyes closed balancing you expand into a grand-plié. Your heels rise off of the hardwood. They call you first, "Brown, Alana Brown. Please take position in center room."

Rose Quartz

Love stone—balances, heals and rejuvenates the emotions. Encourages compassion and harmony

Barefoot

When our daughter falls in love one
Day and grows curious about us,
Wanting our story,
I'd tell her that,
We, both you and I, extinguished that
thing between us,
As if it was a wild fire
That could burn our identities down
That I used to have glimpses of you
In and out of reality
But only in fantasy
Was where we were happy
I was barefoot, in nakedness, dancing
around
Making shapes in sand
All tracing and leading up to you
A you, that eventually soon I couldn't
see anymore
That I remembered a black reflection
in your eyes
That didn't even give me back,

And how at first, like a tide that thing
came
I made you my lifetime
Jumping ahead of God
And I fell, I fell into a realm of my own
fruitless fig trees
And indigo passions,
Where, from that place I loved you…
I loved you …
Like…
A hello
Like a "good morning"
Like fantasy
Like memories of times that used to
Hurt but now can look back at the past
and laugh
I loved you
Like imagination
Like my seeds
Like my grandmother
Like four generations deep
Like another language
Like music
Like honesty
Like wisdom
Like purpose
Like promise
Like poetry

Like prayer
Like earnest prayer
Like answered prayer
Like joy inside of hurt
Like we *are* first spirit beings
Like I am a vessel
Like I am woman
Like I am man with womb
Like, I've been created to birth way
more than babies
I loved you like the inspiration in which
we come from
Like humanity
Like divine order
I loved you like that.
All in my ideas however, before I ever
truly knew you
A premature birth, lungs under-
developed, incubated
Inside of a hopeful little girl's mind
Raised by fairy-tale; the prince saving
her with a kiss otherwise she's lost
There wasn't enough room in desire
for patience
My imagination; shaped by society's
trench
By religious demands

By a ratio analysis of others who were
hasty
Which all boxed me into you.
And you...
A young, unknowing, you
Led by the impulses that your
manhood had yet learned how to
control
Or better yet understand
We twirled around in an unknown
matter
And danced to a rhythm-less beat
Loving, having, creating without
knowing how
We fell dizzy
Fell out of place
Out of context
Never knowing our young minds, dull
Never grabbing
Never... gripping onto...
That chord
That friendship
That awareness of self-
That knowing—one *could* do without
the other
Caged to one another, scratching for
escape,
And so we did... escape

From something we didn't give
enough patience to understand in the
first place
High on image
On ego
On self
We were flame for our drug
It ignited...
Fantasies of us grew trapped in that
hot reality
We extinguished that thing
Heaven and hell went to war because
of us—
An entity so big that earth didn't know
what to do with it.

The Making of Sense

We dance to a rhythm-less beat,
And keep choosing to orbit around
each other.
The question is... why?
Perhaps there's something we,
together,
Do to the earth without knowing.
Soon enough the fruit, or lack thereof
will tell us...

The Connect

Let's twirl around
And together become an unknown
matter
Then, we'll occupy the world
And perhaps we'll understand it just a
bit more

One Accord

When we're together,
On the same frequency,
We change the weather...

2011

Green Eyes

Green eyes!
They found me in a haystack,
Buried deep,
Behind clouds on ground,
Behind flickering stars,
And behind the idea and memory of
her
My indian summer,
I'm scared you're just passing
through,
But if so, I'm prepared to receive what
it is,
That you are to leave with me

Equinox

I love the way you talk to me
It's like nighttime
And you're a wolf howling at the
moon...
Spend the night
Not on beds
Not in rooms
But in another sphere

Oakland

I don't know what it is about you
That found a space in my notebook.
Perhaps it's that
Your rich soil gave way to my seed

Commandment

If you give me anything, give me night
when the moon dances
Give me water
Give me scattered blue, orange and
maroon
It must be fire
Give me poetry…

2010
Indian Summer

Love making to the mind,
Within the realm of your manhood
Inside this place, I'm feeling free
Is there room for me inside of you?

Physical Form

I don't see you anymore
I don't see your image
Or physical substance through eyes
But what I can make out... is God
Beyond my understanding
Through you I see God's love for me
in physical form
I choose this walk with you
Like the autumn leaves walk with the
wind
Later we'll see grey and wrinkled skin
But I'm choosing this walk with you
just like those autumn leaves so
trustingly walk with the wind
In the spirit realm this thing can't bleed
We are in authority like the tallest
mountain choosing to get the rain first
I don't recognize *you* anymore
Or your first approach

Those things that gave me butterflies
Or those tally marks in my unwritten
book of how I pulled your attention
And although we have it
The passion that molded us to this
point right now
Isn't the brightest color
The fireworks no longer the main
attraction
And I don't see just *you* anymore
My optics unable to focus
But what I can make out is...God
Loving me in physical form
Two making things better than when
it's just one
Lifting the other if weak
Intercession when blind
Every fruit of the spirit needed
And beyond what we even think this
love is meant for
There is much...
Wars... in spirit and in natural
Wars against a society mislead that
grabs onto everything that seems like
love
While still abusing it
Us becoming one is like a weapon
arching high like a flamed spear

Penetrating an enemy of mind and
perception
Proving... that there is restoration
That there are second, third, fourth
and forever chances to get it right
It is never too late!
So as we come together
The world won't see us or simply
union anymore
What they will see is God's love for
the world manifested in a physical
form

Rutilated Quartz

*Enhances insight and understanding
of problems, assists in communication
with the higher self*

Mark Ave

A fall night sky warm enough for you
to wear just a white tee. Cognac is
your favorite and it has revved your
engine. You sit on the hood of a car
enjoying the atmosphere—a
celebration. All of your friends and
many you acquaint are here. You
smack and grip hands with others who
come around you. Jokes and laughs
create a magnetic field for more to

partake in the cluster of male camaraderie. They gravitate to you and surprisingly, they do not feel threatened. They feel better about themselves—more handsome, stronger, like one of the cool guys.

The whole block is busy. Many of the girls—the cutest girls here, orbit around you, waiting for eye contact. The moment is heightened with the music. Heads bob and people recite rhymes in unison at certain peaks of each song. In each of those seconds, everyone is connected together, and on the same frequency.

It happens so quickly. No one sees it coming, but somewhere inside you feel it. You are thrown off of the car by a force like a baseball bat hitting you in the neck, and after a few seconds you feel a burning sensation and realize that bullets had hunted you down. They now own you. Your body freezes. For some seconds all you could think of beyond the disorder is how hot the blood feels as it leaks from your neck, drenching your shirt.

All you can see is a blurred spew of images, but feel and hear the frenzy which now is all about *you*. In this chaos, you become a glorified being of society—*this* society's irony. Your body turns into a mass of pressure all of it moving outward. Hot lead finds different cages inside you, thrashing its way around until it rests in a spot that surrenders. You lay frozen while your lungs rage in a war for air. You feel your friend Marcus give you mouth to mouth, begging you to stay in this realm.

You think of your grandmother and how she is expecting you to come home. She always paced the front door for you at nights. Waiting as if she had a feeling of this day coming. Out of all the siblings you have the strongest connection to her—an old little woman, who came over to America with your mother to help raise you. She loves you. "Would this be the thing that killed her in her old age" you thought. Although she did not expand out of the house, or work, or culture herself in Americanism nor become anything more than your nanny—your caretaker, you see how massive of an entity in your world she is. As you spasm in and out of consciousness you feel that it will hurt her the most. Yet still, out of them all your grandmother will handle this with the strongest heart.

You think of your big sister. You know this will shred her. She understands the world you live in and the dangers of just the atmosphere alone. She warned you of this. You see your mother's face, whom like your grandmother doesn't understand your world and cannot counter what you are exposed to. You know she will blame herself. She will do so, because society has to blame someone. So she'll do it first. Thinking of your little sisters who are so young, you grow afraid that they may not be able to handle mourning your loss, and internally you begin to beg for life and for someone to help you. You toil during these minutes with your body and your will. Consciousness becoming less and less yours.

Darkness takes a step in, and you
grow afraid, quickly surrendering to
the fact that this may be your death.
You take this second as an
opportunity that you fear may be lost
and reject all your skepticism or logic,
and beg for a place in Heaven—a
place like the pastor in juvenile hall
had preached to you about. You
refuse to become a being of
nothingness like the darkness
preludes.

Your body lays in the street for
what feels like hours before the

ambulance takes you to the

emergency room. Balloons, candles,

stuffed-animals, cards and empty

alcohol bottles are kept neatly as the

collection increases for months after,

in the spot where your body had laid.

Giant

Lack and Fear
Constructed a deceived people
Bringing him to now speak in silent
pressure
Like dust collected in an untouched
space
And we're looking at it
Seeing a thing a shape with pattern
Familiar headlines,
"Young boy murdered, no suspects"—
police being that suspect
His life; a project with no blue print
Fatherless boy
His mother too broken hearted to hear
the hiss of his enemies at their door
She ain't had no weaponry for him
Like the sun in charge of this universe
Being stripped of its God given ability
to give light, fertilize, to give life
He... stood alone not knowing who or
what he was

Standing in a country declaring him
free
Yet he's caged by past generations
imprint on him
Walking on land mines doing
whatever there is necessary to tread
Given what he has or what he knows
that he has
Blinded
From seeing the indirect cooperation
he plays in killing
Off his own people
And they give him just enough time
To believe in his fabricated glory
In order to build a case against him
That puts him back into a cage
That they never wanted to unleash
him from in the first place
And eventually they came
Busting through mama and grand
mama's house
They be damned if he get anything
without giving them what they claim
The judicial system stripping him of
his manhood
And now he better work hard for little
or get back in it,

All so they can put him right back in
it….
He's drunk inside of the world served
to him
He runs…
Runs from a society that seeks to box
him
A law that wants to cage him
A brother that wants to kill him
A woman that preys upon controlling
him
And from that twisted place in his
understanding; he even wrestles with
his own angles
Federal systems
Media systems
School curriculums
All housing subtle traps of the mind
To indirectly lead him and his brothers
and his sons, and his sons
Like ox to the slaughterhouse
But his spirit must remind him of
What he can't even fight to think of
Remember…
He was that one…
Who found knowledge in a dark room
The one using peace to quench the
hate

Whose desire for a father manifested
into concrete hoop dreams
That one who trucked through a
generation carrying a weight of his
ancestral bloodline, of whom he never
knew—that revolted and fell dead in
an urban jungle
The one who organized
Who marched
Who carried mountains on his back
and gave them supernatural wings,
that took flight in a midnight sky
He loved her
He protected them
He was that one…
So in viewing his shape, or
misperception of what society thinks is
his,
One questions his dynamic to this
space—this world
Praying that his matter take up a
form—indestructible—again, like
before…
Awake our sleeping giant and posses
what's yours

For Anthony *aka Dummy*

I was reluctant to write this piece
Unsure if these words would ripple out
Towards those who walk this earth
dead
And I'm not sure that talking, poems,
or peace rallies
Can do anything for them…
Therefore, I was reluctant to even
write this…
But then I thought about you
And how you carried mountains on
your
Back that took flight
In that December afternoon sky
And how you leave the world with the
gift of your son
And how he was your last thought in
mind
I ask that you let us hug you in our
dreams sometimes

I will never forget the last time that we
spent time
Your eyes are still ours
And I'm not even scared or sad for
you
I know the power that you are in,
Be free our prince
I'm not worried for you or anything
that's
Yours that you leave here
But I am sad for those who walk on
this earth, dead and conditioned
By a master manipulation
I cry for those…
A societal programming that you are
only
A victim of
I pray that you can break free
Your moves are not justified
You die over, and over, and over
inside
And although I am afraid for your soul
I'm looking up in hopes, in
intercession
That the part of you
That's been captured, chained, and
weighed down
Finds rescue…

Your purpose is yours, and you can
have it
Just know that you're bigger than
The force that lies to you

Bringing You Home—The Home of Self

Dear brothers and sisters in prison, I love you. I speak mainly to the brothers at this moment, for it is an urgency of the time for me to do so. Our community suffers. We understand that many of you have done the things to put you in this position, but we know that you were set up. We know this because your father, grandfather, and grandfather's fathers were set up. They want you gone! They want you extinct! However, stay in peace King. If you're reading this it's because you are rising, and as you do, be mindful of the principalities that are at work. They continue to pace about you, waiting for you to open a door to them.

I petition God on your behalf asking
that you gain knowledge. More
importantly, I plead with you to dig for
the understanding as to why such
plots were devised against you. What
is it about you that forced them to
organize ways to confine, keep control
of, breakdown, manipulate, and kill?
What do you posses that they are so
afraid of you using? The answer and
key for liberation from such a system
is within you.
Speaking power and wellness of mind
to you.
A sister

Mark Ave

Empty cognac bottles and balloons;
Your memory still lives.
Had you survived this urban jungle,
Would you have become a lion?

Unakite

Balances the emotional body, and gives awareness of the subconscious blocks. Facilitates the rebirthing process

Dark

I knew by the mini skirt she put on that
it would be just us tonight, again. She
moved hastily from her room to the
bathroom, stepping over and kicking
to the side me and my twin brother's
action figures missing limbs. Gliding
her lipstick on was always the last
step in her process of getting ready.
Matching the pumps, her lips were
glazed with a fire engine red. She left

her makeup and hair products scattered around the bathroom sink. My aunt was at the door. I could tell because she knocked on the metal security gate like she always did, creating a rhythm. Mama gave Ebony permission to unlock and open the door. Ebony was ten, the oldest and was always left in-charge. Twisting the doorknob she opened the door just slightly then returned back towards her space on the carpet in front of the TV, where a fuzzy screen gave way to the evening news.

Baby Jasmine rested on Auntie Dee's hip. A line of smoke from Auntie's cigarette spiraled upward, just missing the baby. Round with curious eyes the baby was still, while the smoke danced around inches from her face. The gate slammed behind Auntie and Mama came out from her room. "I'm ready! I'm ready!" she rushed towards the door. Auntie sat the baby in the middle of Ebony's legs on the floor. "Keep the doors locked! Don't answer for anyone, and keep your eyes on the baby" Mama told Ebony while standing outside waiting for Auntie.

The door closed behind them and we

saw the bottom and top locks turn

from inside. The metal gate slammed.

Michael found a spot on the carpet

right next to Ebony and I inched close

to her as well. We all sat there closely

like a nest of baby birds.

With nothing to watch, Ebony turned

the TV off. The baby started crying

and Ebony went to the cabinet found a

plastic bottle and filled it with milk,

which quickly quieted the little one.

Ebony sat on the couch and started to

rock back and forth patting the baby to sleep. Michael and I rushed to the couch with her. With the TV off and the baby quiet, we could hear every strange noise the apartment walls made. The pounding that I heard from above made me curl closer to Ebony. "It's our neighbors upstairs walking around DANG!" She grew frustrated with me trying to dig underneath her as much as I could. Michael was just as paranoid, but didn't whimper like I did. He just sat still, watching Ebony's move, making sure he stayed close to her. The curtains in the kitchen were too small for the window and I could see darkness from the back patio. I forced myself not to look in that direction. The bushes back there grew larger each year. Spider webs created a film over them. At night it seemed like the bushes grew eyes. I could've sworn one time before, when I looked back there behind the curtains, I saw they had arms and reached out at me. Mama was gone that night too, remembering being too afraid to sleep until the sun came up and her finally

coming home.

The couch, Ebony's right side, and I

started to feel like one, sinking, until

she nudges me to sit up. I wipe the

moisture from the left side of my face.

She nudges Michael too. She leads us

down the hallway toward our room

when everything suddenly goes dark.

Michael and I both grab at Ebony's

elbows as she held the sleeping baby

to her chest with both arms. We all

stood there frozen unable to see

anything. I could tell Ebony was afraid.

I whimpered, thinking of the bushes and their arms. I fear them extending as far as this hallway to grab me like they tried to before. The same thing happened last month, but Mama was home that time. She'd left the next morning to return by noon, and shortly after the lights were back on. The clocks and microwave blinked for a whole week after. Finally, I could see shadows in the walkway. Ebony walked toward our room and we followed.

———————————

The moon reached through the thin weathered sheet nailed over the window giving us enough to see. The only furniture in the room are twin beds and two plastic drawers outlined by the moon's presence. Ebony and the baby laid on her bed and Michael and I jumped under the two sheets on ours. We shared a pillow. I couldn't find that warm sinking feeling again, so I laid there, watching headlights from passing cars make shapes and shadows on the walls.

My heart pounded against the sheets, as the night grew. I wished that I could turn the lights on to help me sleep, but that couldn't happen this night. I tried everything to sneakily keep Michael awake until he started to grow angry and threatened to sleep in Ebony's bed, leaving me by myself. I surrendered, and let his restless toss and turns fade to still.

I grew stiff when I heard keys collide with the metal gate. I spasm relieved that mama was home, to the fear of a stranger possibly being at the door. I melted into the bed, relieved, recognizing Mama's voice—giggles between her and Auntie. "Shit! The power is off. I'm gonna have to go see Dirty in the morning," she slurred her words. There was another voice— deep, a man's. It wasn't any of my uncles or any other man's voice that I knew. A car's headlights outside put a tree branch shadow on the wall which looked like skeleton hands, but I wasn't scared to see it being that Mama was home.

I was warm and sinking until I'd
been poked by the smell of smoke. I
remembered that smell from other
times when Mama came home late
with Auntie. I heard lighter clicks.

"Go easy on that shit baby," the
man said.
Clicks, fire crackling, coughs, and the
three of them clearing their throats
became a pattern—a rhythm that
lullabied me to calm.

———————————

I must have drifted into a dream
when I heard boots plant themselves

at the doorway of our room. It was

dark and I couldn't make out his face.

He was large taking up the doorway.

One side of it caught the man from

stumbling over his feet as he

attempted to take a step in. He rested

to the side of the doorway surveying

the room. I didn't recognize him. I

couldn't see too well in the dark after

having been in a light sleep. My eyes

were almost closed, open just enough

to where I could see his silhouette and

low enough to where he probably

thought I was sleep. He stepped into

our room and closed the door behind him. He staggered to the end of Ebony's bed using his hand to give him balance. I could hear the plastic from my action figure toy crack as he took a few more steps over to the side of her bed. He looked over at Michael and I. I closed my eyes all the way, hoping he couldn't tell that I was awake. He wrestled to find his balance cracking another toy on the ground. Peeking my eyes open, I saw him peel the sheets back from Ebony and the baby. He stood there, hovering over the both of them. They laid there asleep, the baby curled next to Ebony's side. He breathed heavily and grunted in between motions. The side of the bed sunk as he sat down. The bed springs squeaked, waking Ebony. "SShhh pretty. I'm not going to hurt you" he whispered. His breathing grew heavy. Ebony squirmed trying to get under the other end of the sheet that the man had pulled back. He stared at her more intently and slowly drew closer—his body leaning forward like a large boulder on the edge of a cliff.

Ebony whimpered, scooting further up toward the headboard.

My eyes were wide open now. The moon was still in the room, to where I could tell that he wasn't anyone that I had seen before. Based on Ebony's reaction, he was a stranger to her as well. It wasn't her dad because I remember her dad coming by once before, and I recall him being thin. This man was big. The bedsprings hollered as he got all the way on the bed mounting Ebony. She started to cry making small whimpers, kicking her legs against the sheets, as they tangled around her ankles. He sshh'd her and looked into her eyes with a threatening glare. She quieted. She had scooted all the way to the top of the bed, at the headboard and could not scoot away any further from him. He struck a look my way and we caught eyes, his were black and deep. The moon gave his eyes white circles of fire. He slowly put an index finger over his lips, then moved it from one side of his neck to the other. Signaling that he would slice my throat. He peered back down at Ebony. She was shivering, shaking her head no from side to side. The man covered her mouth and leaned in closer to her and I quickly sat up, afraid of what he was going to do to my sister. Reacting to me, he sat up on his knees and gave me a look reminding me of what he had signaled already. On his knees I could see again how big he was. His hands were like catcher's gloves. His belly extended out far in front of him and hung low. "Watch ya self boy!" he said, glaring at me and I shrunk back under my sheet. I wanted to scream but I was afraid of what he might do. "Where was Mama?" I thought.

The baby remained sleep and Michael lay next to me with his mouth wide open drooling on our pillow. Michael was always the last to wake up and if no one forced him he could stay asleep half a day. The man's attention bounced back on Ebony. His chest rattled with each breath as he moved slow and forceful. He had both her hands pinned down above her head with one hand, while the other covered her mouth. He repositioned

himself and I could no longer see her.

He was too large for me to see under

or around him. His belt buckle

clanked. I heard tussling underneath

him for a while then the mattress

bounced and the bedsprings

squeaked, angrily, clawing, and it

went on until finally it stopped.

A Bad Haircut

Dead grass pricked their busy feet. The boy's chubby cheeks were an unquestionable match for the girl's smile— they were a pair. The girl watched over her brother while they played, making sure he didn't pick anything up and put it in his mouth as their mom had instructed. Their mom sat on the concrete side of the yard with her legs crossed on a rust stained white metal patio chair. Khaki shorts framed her petite hourglass figure. The two enjoying their backyard expedition, looked over at her hoping to go further in the yard and she nodded with approval smiling with those eyes—tender and sad. The kids traveled to the worn pinewood fence. Their mom yelled out warning them not to touch it so they wouldn't get splinters. The boy watched his sister intently as she made shapes with small grey stones she'd collected around the yard. The two took conquest of the space—their world which was there's to create and get lost in.

The man from the family picture above the coffee table walked in from the house through the sliding door, and the two kids stood up from their rock creation at the fence. They stared up toward his towering structure. Their eyes grew bright with expectation. Quickly, their mom stood up from her chair scraping the metal against the concrete.

"Since you're really doing this you might as well cut his hair, it's been a month" she walked over and picked her son up swinging him over her hip. "The clippers and shears are in the same place you left them last" she pointed towards inside

the house at a kitchen cabinet.

"Why haven't you brought him

somewhere to maintain his hair?"

"Are you kidding me! that is your

responsibility " she sticks her head out

from her neck as far as it could reach

toward him.

"I didn't come here for this with you. I

have to make this quick, I'm just

stopping by to get a few thin-."

He walked away before finishing his

sentence, ducking as he walked through the

sliding door to the kitchen. Their mom peeked

in the house, then sneakily examined herself

from each of her angles in the window near

the sliding door. Hurriedly, she combed her

fingers through her hair making sure each

strand was intact.

He pushed the patio chair aside scraping

the ground—the metal at war with the concrete,

and set up a toddler high chair. He was set in

what seemed to be one motion. High chair and

clippers plugged into the outlet, shears in his back

pocket, and comb in his right hand. Their mom's

eyes followed his every move, while one arm

cradled the boy over her hip and her lips clenched

tight. He stacked two phone books on the high

chair seat, picked the boy up from his mom's arms and sat him in the chair. "I didn't come here for this" he mumbled. The two year old looked up in his direction, curious, making figure eights, as he followed both of the man's hands prepping. He ran the small-toothed black comb through the hair from back to front and then turned on the clippers. The boy followed the sound—a click, then an angry buzz. The man positions the boy's head. Their mother moved her way into the house and sat at the kitchen table while still looking onto the patio watching—her eyes vapored desolation. Fixedly, the girl watched her brother undergo this process. Chunks of curls fell from the boy's head to the patio ground, while some crept down his face like careful spiders.

"I want one too! I want one too!, I want my haircut" the girl chanted, hopping around in a circle.

The man brushed the boy's face off and lifted him from the high chair onto the ground after finishing.

"Can you give her one too?" their mom begged, rushing her way back into the yard.

"I really have to go" he snapped.

"Look at her! Don't leave her out. Just a little. What... do you have someone waiting for you, is it her?" She fumed. "Ughh, ok damn!" a growl crept from his throat.

He reorganized the high chair in a quick motion. After positioning the girl onto the chair he combed her curls out from her ponytail with his little black comb, pulled all of it between his index and middle finger and told her to look straight ahead. She did just that, and beheld a soft sky tracing a resting sun. She could feel his grip tightening on the ends of her ponytail and heard the shears open. She liked the feel of his grip—his closeness. Sitting in the chair, she drew back to times when she experienced him. A longing for that stirred within her. She remembers times of holding hands, times at the park, and a piggyback ride. Scattered pink, blue, and yellow-orange coat the sky, ushering those memories back to her. The shears closed down on her hair and in an instant the ends of her ponytail fall to the ground, and his grip was gone—the closeness back to distance, again. Her curls along with her brother's rest on the concrete and lay there; same color and texture intertwined.

The man picked the girl up from her armpits, landed a kiss on her forehead and planted her back on the ground. He finds the boy, scoops him up with one arm and kisses twice on his cheeks. Puts him back down with a pat to his head and walks away through the sliding door. His shoulders bullied their way through the entry. Their mother hurried, following him back into the house.

"You will have to find another way to make sure his hair remains cut" he said. never making eye contact.

"So you mean to tell me that you can really walk away… from me, from us, from them!" The vapor from her eyes liquefied.

"There you go. That's why I should have never come, I can't do this right now!" He grabbed a bag of clothes and a typewriter before bulldozing out the front door.

Their mom now sat at the kitchen table with an open bottle of wine and a glass full in front of her. The picture with all of them no longer occupied a space above the coffee table. The sun had made its full departure while the kids made shapes playing in the hair that lay on the concrete.

Jade and Jasper

Protective and grounding. Peaceful and nurturing.

Bedtime

The two little people
Lay on their sides
Facing each other
The air around them chill having been
left alone
They war over space
Where much around them has not
been occupied
The back and forth of sheets
Sounding like a confused wind
That has an affair with fallen leaves
The air grows thicker
The girl threatens to sleep in another
room
And the boy cries out for her stay
His whimper fades like the night grows
Whispers then emerge and ripple
outward
Growing
Giving birth to snickering
Then the buzz of silence
A pattern
Snicker turned bicker
Then the buzz

The moist warmth in their heaviness
now
Reaches out pulling
Toward their damp crowns
Where a kiss finds its rest

Moonstone

Encourages intuitiveness and perception. Enhances the feminine nature

The Woman Roars

I will not accept you
Controlling me
By tethering me to my domestic
duties!
Remember, they are *mine*
As I so choose to have them
Mine to juggle
Mine to execute
Mine to slack at
Mine to master…
I feel no guilt and shame
In allowing the dust in my home to
collect at times
Or spend an entire weekend washing
everything
Including the walls
You will not put constraints
On me, in order for me to feel
validated: like a

"A good woman—A lady"
I'm entrusted to my children
Therefore, God knows
I got this.
Or *God has me* regarding this...
You may find me
In the kitchen making them a hot
breakfast
Sipping coffee
Or at a poetry lounge
Sipping wine
Other times
You'll find me in front of a mirror
Giving my princess two French-braids
Or on a hike all by myself
Away from everyone
Either way
I *am* Woman...
Some days I may even ask my mother
To feed my kids before I make it to
pick them up
Just so I do not have to
And none makes me less of a woman
Or mother...
I do not accept the darts and seeds
You throw toward me
To make me feel
Like anything other

Than a "good woman"
And what is a good woman any way?
Is it one who fits all standards of
beauty,
Intelligence, and skills,
All while being YOURS?
Better yet..
One who's in the house,
Concealed?
How about one who goes above
And beyond to keep you feeling
egotistically safe,
Protecting your pride
Keeping her eyes down
Wearing what you approve, only?
Whatever your definition is
You made it up and
I refuse to accept it!

December 12, 2004 12: something
a.m.
Writing while in a club

Dances on Glass

Open toes
And her beautiful curves
Exposed by skirts
So beautiful is she…
All who come
Come for her
For the chance she silently yet openly
Presents
So beautiful is she…
She takes into her ear
The musical pussy poppin chant
And becomes the night's video queen
So beautiful is she…
Driven by the enemy's gasoline
With exposed frame
Open toe shoes
Broken glass beneath her feet
So beautiful is she…

Onyx Stone

To all the ones who've put up "NO
BLACK WOMEN ALLOWED" signs,
We thank you...
For confirming with us that we have
your attention
For setting the stage perfectly for our
reoccurring debut,
Thank you...
For recognizing that much of our
opposition
Stems from 18th century American
constructs,
Structuring us to be one of the most
disadvantageous individuals within
society

Thank you for reminding us that we are
not soft spoken, for a reason
That we are not "push overs,"

And that our demeanor lines up with
the fact that our domain
Requires us to operate in such
boldness.

Thank you for reminding us that we are
still in battle,
And that our enemies are trying to close
in on us from all sides
We're trucking out of the smoke—
A drugged, lacked, abused, misinformed
couple of hundred years

We're cleaning up the mess.

Some of us,
Have had to listen to the judge sentence
our sons to fifty years of solitude,
While a sister buries her 21 year old.
And we look around, peering through
the dust,
To see that we are holding what they
call "the shorter end of a stick"
Rolling up our sleeves to make moves
towards changing the condition
For a better generation,
All the while they hate us!

Many of us,
Raising families alone,
Embracing and accept it as the way that
it is
Therefore, becoming a mantra,
Which has bread confidence and the
knowing that we can
Tread despite the odds
Getting degrees in our 40's to make
sure
That we can afford for the children to
get them in there 20's
2 jobs, night school, and applications for
every resource available,
All so our daughters can simply enjoy
nature
But time has proven, that despite all of
her degrees, perseverance, and
excellence, they may hate her even
more still,
As the plague from 200 years back tries
to follow
And that's why you see the fire in our
eyes,
Which frightens you...

But fear not!
We're just thinking
We're just planning
For escape
From such a construct
That we may be able to give back to this
earth
A deposit of this fire
Torching the matrilineal passion within
every woman
So that she may recognize that she is
both
The High priestess and a General
Where no power
Can manipulate or control

Her counterpart should be very afraid
But fear not
She is the portal
She is the signage on your path
She is the clairsentience of your solar
plexus chakra
She's your white owl
She's the wolf in your pack
She is your new and full moon
She is the aesthetic truth

NO! You will no longer lie to her
You will not separate yourself from her
You will not divide her from her dark
skin, brown skin,
light skin,
And all other races of sisters
You will no longer ban her
Because now you know her
Therefore, to all of the ones who put up
"NO BLACK WOMEN ALLOWED" signs
We thank you!

79092675R00067

Made in the USA
Columbia, SC
26 October 2017